CHAPTER 1: THE DEALERSHIP ADVANTAGE: THE BENEFITS OF THE DEALERSHIP

I n the modern automotive landscape, the complexity of vehicles has reached unprecedented heights. With intricate technologies and interwoven systems, today's cars pose challenges that demand specialized knowledge and expertise. When it comes to entrusting your vehicle to capable hands, the question arises: Why choose the dealership? In this chapter, we delve deep into the myriad advantages that dealerships offer, exploring their unmatched value in servicing and maintaining your cherished automobile.

Mastery Over Complexity

The intricacies of modern vehicles can leave even seasoned mechanics scratching their heads. Independent shops, while proficient in handling a wide array of vehicles, might encounter situations where a particular issue exceeds their capabilities. As a result, the vehicle is often rerouted to a dealership for resolution. However, this route incurs unnecessary time and costs, ultimately passed on to the vehicle owner.

Dealerships boast technicians who are specifically trained to navigate the complexities of the vehicles they service. Their in-depth familiarity with the intricacies of various makes and models enables them to diagnose and rectify problems with pinpoint accuracy. Choosing the dealership ensures that your vehicle is handled by professionals with unmatched expertise in handling the challenges posed by modern automotive technology.

The Advantage of Experience

Imagine seeking medical attention from a general practitioner for a specialized ailment, when a specialist is readily available. Similarly, opting for an independent

shop can be likened to choosing a "jack of all trades." Dealerships, on the other hand, specialize in the specific vehicles they represent. This specialization translates to a wealth of experience in diagnosing and resolving issues unique to those vehicles.

Dealership technicians encounter a consistent stream of vehicles similar to yours, allowing them to recognize patterns and identify potential problems swiftly. This familiarity with common issues, along with access to manufacturer databases and technical updates, empowers them to tackle challenges effectively, often resolving them in a fraction of the time it might take an independent shop to do so.

Technological Prowess

In an era defined by rapid technological advancement, vehicles have evolved into complex machines intertwined with cutting-edge technology. From adaptive cruise control to intricate engine management systems, the modern car's inner workings demand a comprehensive understanding of both mechanical and digital components. Dealerships stand at the forefront of this technological evolution.

Equipped with the latest diagnostic tools and software, dealership technicians possess the means to access real-time data from your vehicle's onboard computer systems. This direct access to the heart of your car's digital infrastructure expedites the diagnostic process, enabling technicians to identify issues swiftly and accurately. With the ability to diagnose, update, and recalibrate your vehicle's software, dealerships are equipped to keep your car running optimally in the face of ever-advancing technology.

Trained Excellence

Dealerships prioritize continuous training and development for their technicians. This commitment to excellence ensures that dealership staff is well-versed in the latest advancements and techniques pertinent to the vehicles they service. As vehicles become more intricate and integrated, technicians need to stay abreast of evolving technology, and dealerships invest heavily in training to fulfill this need.

The rigorous training programs offered by dealerships enable technicians to earn certifications that validate their expertise. These certifications are often granted by manufacturers, attesting to the technician's proficiency in handling specific models. As a result, you can be confident that the technician working on your vehicle has undergone comprehensive training and possesses the necessary skills to address even the most intricate issues. We will get into this more in later chapters.

Economic Efficiency

Contrary to popular belief, dealership services can be surprisingly economical, especially for certain tasks. While independent shops often need to cover their overhead costs by marking up prices on routine maintenance services, dealerships can offer competitive prices for these services. Dealerships view maintenance as a crucial aspect of their business, and they understand that attracting customers with cost-effective maintenance can lead to long-term relationships. Also, they make money from the manufacturers' warranties and can discount what they call customer-paying work because of that.

Moreover, dealerships can offer genuine manufacturer parts that are specifically designed for your vehicle. These parts not only ensure optimal performance but also come with warranties that safeguard your investment. While independent shops might opt for aftermarket parts to save costs, dealerships prioritize your vehicle's longevity and performance by providing parts that meet the manufacturer's standards.

Holistic Care

Dealerships provide comprehensive care that extends beyond mere repairs. They are equipped to address recalls, special coverages which is a repair free to you that might address your issue, software updates, and warranty issues efficiently and effectively. When your vehicle visits a dealership, you can be certain that all aspects of its well-being are being attended to under one roof. This holistic approach to maintenance and service ensures that your vehicle remains in top condition, upholding its safety, performance, and value.

In conclusion, the choice to entrust your vehicle to a dealership is a decision rooted in wisdom and pragmatism. The mastery over complexity, the advantage of experience, technological prowess, trained excellence, economic efficiency, and holistic care all converge to form a compelling case for dealership services. In an automotive landscape defined by innovation and intricacy, dealerships stand as beacons of expertise, poised to provide unparalleled service that befits the modern automobile's intricate nature.

CHAPTER 2: DEMYSTIFYING THE DEALERSHIP SERVICE PROCESS: HOW IT FLOWS

I n the intricate world of dealership service, the process of transforming a vehicle from a state of concern to a condition of optimal performance involves a well-orchestrated series of steps. This chapter delves into the inner workings of this process, offering you a comprehensive understanding of how things run behind the scenes. While variations might exist between dealerships, the fundamental principles of this process remain constant, ensuring that your vehicle's issues are addressed efficiently and effectively.

Initiating the Journey: The Advisor's Role

Your journey through the dealership service process commences with the advisor. As the bridge between you and the technical team, the advisor is responsible for understanding your concerns and conveying them accurately to the technicians. This crucial step hinges on effective communication, as your description of the issue serves as the foundation upon which the entire process is built. Bring as much information as possible and make sure it gets relayed to the technician by the advisor.

Upon receiving your vehicle, the advisor meticulously records your concerns and inputs them into the dealership's system. This step is pivotal, as it initiates the process and ensures that your vehicle's issues are properly documented and tracked. The advisor also assesses the urgency of the situation, determining whether your vehicle requires immediate attention or can be scheduled for a later date. They should be asking you all types of questions; they should not be "order takers" but getting all the information the technician will need to help him solve your issues.

Directing the Flow: Handing Off to the Dispatcher

Once your concerns are documented, the advisor passes the proverbial baton to the dispatcher. Some shops will have the advisors dispatch their work and have a team system in place.

The dispatcher's role is akin to that of an air traffic controller, strategically allocating vehicles to technicians based on various factors. If an issue is time-sensitive or requires specialized expertise, the dispatcher might assign it to a technician who can address it promptly. On the other hand, if the best-suited technician is momentarily backed up with work, the dispatcher might opt for a slightly delayed assignment, often leading to more meticulous attention.

The dispatcher's skill lies in resource allocation and timeline management. By assessing the workload of each technician, considering their areas of expertise, and accounting for the urgency of issues, the dispatcher orchestrates an efficient flow of work that minimizes delays and maximizes quality.

The Technician's Expertise: Estimation and Execution

With the assignment in hand, the technician takes center stage. Drawing on their training and experience, the technician conducts a thorough assessment of your vehicle. This evaluation involves diagnosing the issue, identifying potential root causes, and formulating a plan of action. If specialized tools or equipment are required, the technician ensures their availability before proceeding.

Having diagnosed the issue, the technician estimates the cost of repairs, encompassing both labor and parts. If it is a manufacture warranty repair, he will update the advisor and proceed with ordering parts or performing the repair. This estimate is a crucial step that informs you of the anticipated expenses associated with resolving the problem. Once the estimate is prepared, it is submitted to the advisor for review and subsequent communication with you.

Advisor Engagement: Presenting the Estimate

The advisor plays a pivotal role in facilitating communication between you and the technical team. Armed with the technician's estimate, the advisor reaches out to you, either through a phone call or in-person consultation. During this interaction, the advisor provides a detailed breakdown of the estimate, explaining the necessary repairs, associated costs, and potential consequences of delaying or declining the service.

Your approval or declination of the estimate is a significant juncture in the process. If you approve, the technician proceeds with the repairs, utilizing genuine manufacturer' parts and their technical expertise to restore your vehicle to its optimal state. However, if you decline the estimate, the process takes a different route, as the technician's efforts shift toward preparing the vehicle for your departure.

Resolution and Beyond: Execution and Documentation

Upon receiving your approval, the technician gets to work, executing the repairs as outlined in the estimate. This stage requires precision and meticulous attention to detail, as the technician endeavors to restore your vehicle's functionality to factory standards. Whether it involves complex engine diagnostics or intricate software updates, the technician's expertise comes to the forefront, ensuring that your vehicle receives the care it deserves.

If you decline the estimate, the technician's role pivots toward preparing a detailed report outlining the issues identified, the declined services, and any potential consequences of neglecting the repairs. This report serves as a valuable record, not only for your reference but also for future visits or evaluations of your vehicle. No matter if the repairs were approved or declined the technician will document his findings and actions in the repair order.

Journey's End: Delivering Quality Service

As the technician's efforts culminate in either successful repairs or a thorough report, the advisor takes the reins once more. Upon confirming the quality of the service, the advisor arranges for the return of your vehicle, accompanied by a detailed summary of the work performed.

Should you have opted to decline the repairs, the advisor

communicates the declined services and provides guidance on the potential consequences of delaying or neglecting them. This transparent communication empowers you to make informed decisions about your vehicle's maintenance and well-being.

Beyond the Process: Building Trust and Satisfaction
While this chapter outlines the step-by-step process of dealership service, it's important to recognize that the journey doesn't end here. Dealerships prioritize customer satisfaction and aim to foster trust and long-term relationships. The successful execution of the service process, coupled with open communication, expertise, and dedication, contributes to your overall dealership experience, paving the way for future visits and addressing your automotive needs.

In summary, the process of dealership service is a symphony of coordination, expertise, and communication. From the initial input of concerns by the advisor to the technician's diagnosis and execution of repairs, every step is orchestrated with the aim of restoring your vehicle to its peak performance. This comprehensive understanding of the service process equips you with the knowledge to navigate the dealership experience confidently and effectively.

CHAPTER 3: OPTIMAL MAINTENANCE: AVOIDING BUYING UNNECESSARY MAINTENANCE KNOWING YOUR OWNER'S MANUAL.

Maintaining your vehicle in prime condition is a responsibility that goes hand in hand with car ownership. As vehicles age, various components require attention to ensure their longevity and optimal performance. In the quest to keep your vehicle running smoothly, the key lies in following the guidance outlined in your owner's manual. A lot of dealerships have moved from the owner's manual to products and services that they can make more money on and do more frequently. This chapter delves into the importance of adhering to manufacturer-recommended maintenance schedules and materials, offering insights into the pitfalls of deviating from these guidelines and venturing into uncharted automotive territories.

The Manufacturer's Blueprint: Your Owner's Manual

Your vehicle's owner's manual is more than just a booklet stuffed in your glove compartment. It's a comprehensive guide meticulously crafted by the manufacturer, outlining the most effective means to care for your vehicle. From oil change intervals to tire rotations and from fluid specifications to component replacements, the owner's manual encapsulates a wealth of knowledge tailored to your specific make and model.

Manufacturer-recommended maintenance schedules are not arbitrary; they're based on extensive research, testing, and engineering. These schedules are designed to maximize the lifespan of your vehicle while ensuring optimal performance and safety. Deviating from these guidelines can potentially lead to premature wear, reduced fuel efficiency, and compromised safety. Performing these slightly early is a good thing. For instance, I do not do my oil change at the manufacturer 7,500-mile recommendation but instead every 5k. My transmission service is due every 45k miles I will do around 40k. A top engine induction service GM recommends every other oil change I do every other oil change. I am a fan of this service as anyone who has seen carboned up valves should be.

The Temptation of Additives and Aftermarket Fluids

In a marketplace flooded with various automotive products, it's easy to be enticed by the promises of additives and aftermarket fluids. This chapter and topic will likely drum up a lot of talk on both sides. I will say as a certified technician and working for a dealership for 22 years I have not used any of these on my personal vehicle and I stick to the manufacturer fluids and cleaners. These products often claim to enhance performance, increase fuel efficiency, and even extend the life of your vehicle's components. However, it's crucial to approach such products with a discerning eye. A lot of these are pushed on the dealership by these companies with dollar signs. Advisors get spiffs and so do technicians for doing them.

Manufacturers invest substantial resources in engineering their vehicles and the fluids that go into them. The fluids specified in your owner's manual are formulated to meet precise requirements, ensuring compatibility with your vehicle's intricate systems. Additives and aftermarket fluids might not align with these specifications, potentially leading to adverse reactions, reduced performance, or even damage to critical components.

I am not here to say these additives etc. do not work, but I know the manufacturer I work for does not recommend using them. Personally, I do not use them and not many techs I know do.

Uncharted Services: Beyond Manufacturer Recommendations
What I want to bring to your attention is that a lot of times these cleaners and additives do not align with your owner's manual recommendations, and you can end up spending a lot more money following these service recommendations. As you navigate the automotive landscape, you might encounter service centers that recommend maintenance services not outlined in your owner's manual. These services often fall under the guise of "extra care" or "extended protection." While some of these services might provide a marginal benefit, it's essential to consider the intent behind them.

Deviating from manufacturer recommendations can lead to several pitfalls. Not only might you spend money on services that don't offer substantial benefits, but you could also inadvertently void your vehicle's warranty. Manufacturers are explicit in their recommendations for one reason: to ensure that your vehicle maintains its optimal performance and safety over time. You would not think dealerships would use these other services, but they do often.

Factory Fluids: The Gold Standard

Factory fluids, also known as original equipment manufacturer (OEM) fluids, are designed with your vehicle's unique specifications in mind. These fluids undergo rigorous testing to meet precise standards set by the manufacturer. Using factory fluids is akin to giving your vehicle the nourishment it requires to function optimally.

Contrastingly, some service centers might offer flushes or fluid replacements that don't align with the manufacturer's recommendations. While these services might seem appealing, they can introduce foreign substances into your vehicle's systems, potentially causing more harm than good. Vehicles are becoming way pickier about fluids and just using the wrong oil can cause anything from check engine lights to other issues.

Staying Aligned: Manufacturer and Maintenance

While adhering to the manufacturer's maintenance schedule is crucial, it's worth noting that some adjustments can be made. For instance, performing oil changes slightly earlier than recommended, especially if you frequently drive in challenging conditions, can offer added protection to your engine. However, any modifications to the schedule should be made with careful consideration and in consultation with a knowledgeable professional.

The Path to Longevity and Performance

In a world where shortcuts and quick fixes are often sought after, taking the path of diligence and adherence to manufacturer guidelines is a testament to your commitment to your vehicle's longevity and performance. Your owner's manual is more than a reference—it's a roadmap to maintaining your investment in top-notch condition.

Ultimately, the choice to follow manufacturer-recommended

maintenance and materials is a choice to prioritize quality, safety, and your vehicle's long-term well-being. In an era where vehicles are becoming increasingly sophisticated, placing your trust in the wisdom of the manufacturer is a surefire way to keep your vehicle running smoothly, efficiently, and safely for years to come. Just let them know if it is not in the owner's manual, it's not for you. Of course, that is your decision and whatever decision you make just be aware of both sides.

CHAPTER 4:
NAVIGATING
TECHNICIANS:
THE VALUE OF AN
EXPERIENCED HAND

When it comes to entrusting your vehicle to the hands of a technician, experience and expertise matter more than you might realize. The complexities of modern vehicles require a skilled touch, and not all technicians are created equal. This chapter dives deep into the crucial aspect of choosing or should I say requesting an experienced technician to diagnose and resolve your vehicle's issues. By understanding the tiers of technician expertise and the impact of this choice, you can save time, money, and avoid potential headaches in the long run.

The Spectrum of Expertise: A, B, and C-Level Technicians

Dealerships employ a range of technicians, often classified into different levels of expertise denoted as A, B, and C. These distinctions are not just mere titles; they reflect varying degrees of experience, training, and competency. At the apex stands the A-level technician, boasting extensive training, years of hands-on experience, and an in-depth understanding of the intricacies of various vehicle systems.

In the middle ground reside the B-level technicians. They possess a commendable level of proficiency, though not at the same caliber as their A-level counterparts. On the other end of the spectrum are the C-level technicians. These technicians, often in the early stages of their career, are still honing their skills and might not possess the same depth of expertise as more seasoned colleagues. A good C level utilizing his dealership resources and peers can still be very effective.

The Challenge of Diagnosis: Experience Matters

One of the most critical phases in vehicle service is diagnosis— the process of identifying the root cause of a problem. This phase requires a profound understanding of vehicle systems, an ability to decipher complex error codes, and the intuition to connect seemingly unrelated symptoms to their underlying issues. A-level technicians excel in this domain, often capable of swiftly and accurately diagnosing problems that might leave their less experienced counterparts stumped.

Consider a scenario where your vehicle exhibits an unusual noise when accelerating. An A-level technician might recognize the distinct sound pattern, pinpoint its source, and recommend a solution promptly. In contrast, a C-level technician might struggle with the diagnosis, leading to extended hours of labor, trial and error, and potential misdiagnosis. The expertise of an experienced technician can mean the difference between a swift resolution and a prolonged ordeal.

The Financial Implication: Efficient Repairs, Lower Costs

It's no secret that labor costs are a significant component of vehicle service expenses. Opting for an experienced technician can significantly impact these costs. A-level technicians possess the knowledge to diagnose and address issues efficiently, leading to shorter labor times. This efficiency translates into reduced costs, as you're not paying for extended hours of experimentation or redundant repairs.

Imagine a situation where a less experienced technician takes hours to diagnose a problem that an A-level technician could identify in minutes. The unnecessary labor costs associated with the former scenario can be avoided by choosing a technician who possesses the necessary experience to tackle the problem head-on. Regardless of you should not have to pay for the less experienced technicians training and struggles that should be at his cost or the dealerships. Unfortunately, that is not always the case.

Ensuring Quality and Reliability: Preventing Return Visits

When a technician lacks the experience to identify the core issue, the likelihood of a problem returning is significantly higher. This not only leads to additional inconvenience but also increases your expenses. Return visits due to unresolved or misdiagnosed issues can sour your dealership experience and leave you questioning the competence of the service center.

An experienced technician reduces the likelihood of repeat visits. By accurately diagnosing and addressing problems, they minimize the chances of lingering issues or complications arising from incomplete repairs. This not only saves you time but also preserves your peace of mind, knowing that your vehicle has been comprehensively serviced by a knowledgeable professional.

Navigating the Technician Selection Process

Ensuring that your vehicle is in the hands of an experienced technician requires proactive communication with your service advisor. When discussing your vehicle's issues, explicitly request that an experienced technician handles the diagnosis and repair. This can be as simple as adding a line to your repair order, emphasizing your preference for an experienced technician.

The role of the service advisor is pivotal in ensuring your preferences are communicated to the dispatcher. This step ensures that the right technician is assigned to your vehicle, setting the stage for a more efficient and successful service experience. Remember these technicians might be slammed with work so it might take a little longer to get it to them.

The Wise Choice for Peace of Mind

Choosing an experienced technician is not just about technical competence; it's about peace of mind. When your vehicle is in the hands of a professional with a wealth of experience, you can rest assured that every aspect of the diagnosis and repair process is being conducted with precision and care. Your vehicle deserves nothing less than the expertise that an A-level or B-level technician can provide. As stated, if a C level properly utilizes his resources and peers he can be just as effective. I was at C level once and strived and excelled quickly. Regardless, the good thing about dealerships is they will own up to any mistakes that they or the technicians make. Most have policy accounts that get high every month. Getting a C tech is not a bad thing, but at the same time they are the riskier choice and can cost you a lot if the dealership isn't paying attention and you do not understand the basics and do not ask questions.

In conclusion, the importance of selecting an experienced technician cannot be overstated. From efficient diagnosis to cost savings and the prevention of return visits, the advantages of choosing an A-level or B-level technician are abundant. By understanding the distinctions between technician tiers and actively requesting experienced hands, you empower yourself to make informed choices that contribute to the longevity, performance, and reliability of your beloved vehicle.

CHAPTER 5: MASTERING DEALERSHIP NEGOTIATION AND ESTIMATE TIPS

Negotiating with a dealership might seem like a daunting task, but armed with the right knowledge and strategies, you can ensure that you're getting the best value for your vehicle's maintenance and repairs. This chapter explores the art of spot-checking, price matching, and the importance of thorough estimate examination when dealing with a dealership or any repair facility for that matter. These tactics empower you to navigate the service experience with confidence and financial savvy.

Price Check Your Way to Savings

When it comes to vehicle maintenance and repairs, knowledge is your greatest ally. Dealerships operate in a competitive marketplace, and their pricing can vary. One effective strategy is to compare prices among competitive dealerships in your area. While dealerships might not view independent garages or tire stores as direct competitors, they certainly view other dealerships as rivals.

Spend a little time and call to get prices from different dealerships for the same service or repair. Ensure that you're comparing "apples to apples," meaning that the services, parts, and labor included in the estimate are identical. This approach allows you to gauge the competitiveness of the dealership's pricing and potentially negotiate for a better deal.

The Power of Price Matching

Dealerships, like any business, value customer loyalty. If you present a lower estimate from a competing dealership for the same service, many dealerships will be willing to price match. This can be especially advantageous if you prefer one dealership over another due to factors such as location, convenience, or prior positive experiences.

However, exercise caution when employing this tactic. Some less reputable establishments might initially provide a lower estimate to entice you but later inflate costs once you're committed. To avoid this pitfall, ensure that the estimate you're comparing is detailed and comprehensive. Transparency is key.

Negotiation: A Valuable Tool

While negotiation might not be the first thing that comes to mind when dealing with a dealership, it's a valuable tool at your disposal. Dealerships are often open to some degree of negotiation, especially when presented with a reasonable request. Remember that negotiation isn't about trying to get something for nothing; it's about arriving at a fair and equitable arrangement. Some might stand by it and say no, but price matching is a reasonable request.

Asking for a breakdown of parts and labor or inquiring about the labor time guide used by technicians' signals to the dealership that you're a savvy customer who's serious about paying only for justified expenses. This transparency and attention to detail can encourage dealerships to provide you with a more accurate estimate without padding it. Believe it or not, if you have an extended warranty that is how they approve estimates. They make sure they are only approving labor time from a well-known time guide and that parts are the correct price.

Time Guides and Labor Estimates

When a technician creates an estimate, the labor component should be based on established time guides. These guides, developed by industry standards organizations, provide recommended labor times for various repairs and services. Requesting information about which time guide the dealership uses not only demonstrates your commitment to a fair assessment but also ensures that the labor component of your estimate is justifiable. As stated before, that is what extended warranty companies use so this is common talk inside a service center, but rarely heard from the everyday customer.

By making the dealership aware that you have a knowledge of time guides and will thoroughly review the estimate and invoice, you create an environment where they are more likely to provide a transparent and accurate assessment. These time guides usually require a subscription to access so getting access may not be feasible for everyone. You might get close online, but the point here is to just mention it. This not only benefits you as the customer but also ensures that the dealership maintains ethical business practices.

Wisdom in Estimate Examination

Whether you're a seasoned automotive enthusiast or a first-time vehicle owner, a wise approach to estimate examination is invaluable. Scrutinize every element of the estimate to ensure that it aligns with the services required for your vehicle's maintenance or repair. A well-justified estimate should include all necessary components, leaving no room for guesswork or ambiguity.

If you encounter discrepancies or uncertainties in the estimate, don't hesitate to seek clarification from the dealership. An open dialogue can help you gain a better understanding of the services being provided and their associated costs. This ensures that you're only paying for what is genuinely necessary.

The Balancing Act: Negotiation Wisdom

While negotiation can be a valuable tool in your automotive toolkit, it's essential to strike a balance. Dealerships, like any business, need to maintain their profitability to provide quality service and employ skilled technicians. Excessive negotiation can lead to a strained relationship, inflated estimates in anticipation of haggling, or, in extreme cases, refusal of service.

Use negotiation wisely, reserving it for instances where you genuinely believe that a better deal is attainable, or when faced with an estimate that seems unreasonable. Strive for fair and transparent communication, working together with the dealership to arrive at a mutually beneficial solution.

A Strategic Approach to Dealership Service

In conclusion, spot checking, price matching, and negotiation are powerful tools in your arsenal for navigating dealership service experiences. By comparing estimates, asking for transparency, and negotiating thoughtfully, you can ensure that you're receiving quality service at a fair price. Remember that your goal is not just to save money but also to establish a constructive and transparent relationship with the dealership, where both parties benefit from fair and equitable transactions.

CHAPTER 6: INQUIRE ABOUT MANUFACTURER REBATES AND COUPONS

I n the realm of dealership service, there's a treasure trove of savings just waiting to be discovered through manufacturer rebates and dealership coupons. Surprisingly, a significant number of these opportunities often go unused. Managers will usually throw any rebate material to hang up in a corner in their office, and coupons stay on the website without any mention to the customer. This chapter unveils the secrets of these money-saving gems and shares insights on how to leverage them to optimize your vehicle maintenance and repair costs.

The Hidden World of Manufacturer Rebates

Manufacturer rebates represent a common way for automakers to encourage vehicle owners to invest in their vehicle's maintenance and repair with genuine parts and services. These rebates span a wide array of items, including filters, tires, engines, and more. They are frequently updated, often on a monthly or quarterly basis, offering savings opportunities across various vehicle components to drive business.

The surprising aspect is that many of these valuable rebates often go unnoticed. Service managers may accumulate rebate information. When they get the material to put up around the dealership in the middle of a busy day it gets sat in the office. While service advisors might not always stay up to date on the latest offerings. This results in missed opportunities for vehicle owners to save money. One thing I always made sure of was to go over these with the advisors and put up the material for the customers, but I found that to be rare. Always ask. As I am writing this GM had summer long rebates on Air Filters, Batteries, Brakes, and Wipers. $10 per filter, $15 for wipers, $40 for Brake pads, $40 for Brake rotors and $20 for Batteries. I bet a lot of people bought these services and needed them during that time but were never made aware of rebate and the 2-minute process to fill out the paperwork online. Every manufacturer is different, Ford right now is offering $100 Tire rebate on multiple brands. They are also giving bonus reward points on some services. GM has a point system as well for services. These are all the systems you must get signed up for and see your dealer to do so.

The Straightforward Process of Rebate Redemption

The good news is that redeeming manufacturer rebates is often a straightforward process. Many rebates can be claimed by vehicle owners through simple means, including mail-in forms or even easier online submission forms that take only a few minutes of your time. The key is to be aware of what rebates are available and take the initiative to claim them. I have walked many customers through a two-minute process and have saved them hundreds of dollars on needed maintenance and repairs.

Keep in mind that rebate eligibility criteria and deadlines may vary, so it's essential to read the fine print and ensure you meet all requirements. The savings you can obtain through manufacturer rebates can be substantial, making it a worthwhile endeavor. If you do not see signage of up to date rebates the odds are someone will have to do some digging to find out what is out there. Sad to say I know managers that might not even know how to find out. Do some digging for yourself, it could pay off well on your visit. Being a service advisor and manager is a very busy job, so I am not knocking them if they do not keep up and know what's out there. Then again, I believe they should and recommend you ask and dug yourself in case they do not.

Dealership Coupons: A Hidden Trove

Dealerships frequently offer coupons for various services and components. These coupons can significantly reduce your vehicle maintenance and repair costs and are often readily available on dealership websites. However, they often go unnoticed because vehicle owners assume that dealerships automatically apply these discounts.

Unless you actively seek out these coupons, they might not

be mentioned during the busy daily operations of the service department. By being proactive and inquiring about available coupons, you can uncover valuable opportunities to save money. I have seen customers pay full price for something and there was a coupon out on it. I stop it whenever I see it or can, but always check and ask.

The Advisor's Role: A Key to Savings

The effectiveness of tapping into manufacturer rebates and coupons often hinges on the diligence of your service advisor. A proactive service advisor who stays updated on the latest rebates and coupons can be your gateway to significant savings. If you find an advisor who goes the extra mile to inform you about these money-saving opportunities, consider it a valuable partnership. I love to see my advisors on top of these things and letting customers know.

On the flip side, if you're a service advisor reading this, it's crucial to recognize that your efforts in saving customers money do not go unnoticed. By taking the initiative to inform customers about available rebates and coupons, you not only enhance their service experience but also build trust and loyalty. A satisfied customer is more likely to return for future service needs.

Navigating the Hidden Savings Landscape

To unlock the hidden savings potential of manufacturer rebates and coupons, take a proactive approach:

- **Ask Your Service Advisor:** When scheduling your vehicle for service or repairs, don't hesitate to ask your service advisor about any available manufacturer rebates or dealership coupons. They should be able to provide you with the most up-to-date information.
- **Check the Dealership Website:** Dealerships often post coupons on their websites. Before your visit, take a few minutes to explore their online offers and take note of any relevant coupons.
- **Stay Informed:** Keep yourself informed about your

vehicle's maintenance schedule and recommended service intervals. This knowledge will help you identify opportunities to take advantage of rebates and coupons when servicing is due.

- **Review Rebate Eligibility:** If you plan to purchase specific parts or components for your vehicle, review the manufacturer's rebate eligibility criteria in advance. This proactive approach ensures you meet all requirements when it's time to claim your rebate.

Beyond Savings: The Added Benefits

Uncovering manufacturer rebates and dealership coupons isn't just about reducing your expenses. It's also about maximizing the value you receive for your investment in vehicle maintenance and repair. By actively seeking out these opportunities, you not only save money but also demonstrate a commitment to caring for your vehicle with the best quality parts and services available.

In summary, manufacturer rebates and dealership coupons represent the hidden treasures of dealership service. With a proactive approach and the assistance of a knowledgeable service advisor, you can unearth these savings opportunities, ultimately enhancing your vehicle ownership experience while keeping your costs in check. Your manufacturer may not have any of the above, but it would be worth the short amount of time to check. Vehicle repairs like everything today can get costly.

CHAPTER 7: MANUFACTURER ASSISTANCE: THE HIDDEN SAVINGS FOR POST-WARRANTY REPAIRS

M any vehicle owners are unaware of the potential lifeline that manufacturers can offer when it comes to out-of-warranty repairs. While the policies and assistance levels may vary among manufacturers, this chapter reveals a little-known secret in the automotive world: manufacturers may aid with post-warranty repairs, offering valuable savings for loyal customers.

Manufacturer Assistance: A Well-Kept Secret

The concept of manufacturer assistance for post-warranty repairs often eludes many vehicle owners. It's not widely advertised, and unless you specifically inquire about it, you might miss out on potential savings. Most manufacturers have some form of assistance policy in place, but the terms and conditions can differ.

Loyalty Pays Off

One of the key factors that manufacturers consider when offering assistance is customer loyalty. They may consider how many vehicles you've purchased from the brand and how frequently you've visited the dealership for service. The more loyal you are to the brand, the more likely you are to receive assistance.

This loyalty-based approach is a win-win situation. Manufacturers reward their dedicated customers with cost savings, and customers benefit from potential financial assistance during the repair process.

The Assistance Algorithm

Manufacturers often employ an algorithm to determine the level of assistance they provide. This algorithm factors in various elements, such as your loyalty to the brand, the nature of the repair, and how far out of warranty. The result is a percentage of the repair cost that the manufacturer is willing to cover. Some manufacturers just leave it in management's hands, each will differ.

The assistance percentage is typically applied to the repair at warranty rates, which are generally more affordable than standard repair rates. This can significantly reduce the overall cost of the repair.

The Critical Savings Factor

Manufacturer assistance can be a game-changer when you're faced with a significant repair bill just outside your warranty period. Even if the manufacturer covers only a portion of the cost

—say, 10% to 20%—this discount, combined with the reduced warranty rates, can make a substantial dent in your repair expenses.

This is precisely why maintaining a history of dealership service can be beneficial. Loyalty to the brand and consistent servicing at the dealership can increase your chances of receiving manufacturer assistance when it matters most.

Timing Is Key

While you can inquire about manufacturer assistance at any time, it's advisable to do so strategically. It's generally more effective to request assistance for a substantial repair that falls slightly outside your warranty period. Manufacturers may track instances of assistance, and frequent requests might lead to reduced assistance percentages in the future.

The Art of Requesting Assistance

Requesting manufacturer assistance is relatively straightforward. You can approach your service manager and express your interest in exploring this option for your repair. The service manager will typically enter the relevant information online, and the manufacturer will evaluate your request.

Remember that this is not a guaranteed service, and the manufacturer's decision is based on a variety of factors. However, your chances of receiving assistance increase with a history of loyalty to the brand and the dealership.

An Added Layer of Peace of Mind

Manufacturer assistance is not only about financial savings but also about peace of mind. Knowing that you have a potential ally in the form of the manufacturer when facing a significant repair can alleviate the stress associated with unexpected vehicle expenses. It underscores the value of maintaining a strong relationship with your dealership and staying loyal to the brand.

In conclusion, manufacturer assistance is a hidden gem in the realm of post-warranty vehicle repairs. By inquiring strategically and maintaining loyalty to the brand and dealership, you can tap into this valuable resource, potentially saving a significant amount of money when it matters most. It's a testament to the benefits of building a long-term relationship with your vehicle manufacturer and dealer.

CHAPTER 8: CREATE A RELATIONSHIP: POSITIVE RELATIONSHIPS CAN HAVE A BIG IMPACT

In the realm of dealership service, forging a positive and enduring relationship with the people who work there can be your ultimate asset. This chapter explores the profound advantages of creating a meaningful connection with your local dealership, illustrating how such a relationship can led to financial benefits, enhanced service experiences, and a sense of trust that money can't buy. This will most likely hold true to anyone who works on your vehicle or other aspects in life.

Beyond the Transactional

At its core, a relationship with your local dealership transcends the transactional nature of business. It's about cultivating a rapport with the individuals who manage, service, and repair your vehicle. When you move beyond the purely transactional aspect, you unlock a world of possibilities.

The Power of Recognition

When you're a familiar face at the dealership, you're more than just a customer—you're a valued part of their community. This recognition often leads to several significant benefits:

- **Discounts and Special Offers:** Advisors and service managers may go the extra mile by offering discounts or special deals to customers they know and appreciate. These gestures can translate into substantial savings over time.
- **Extra Mile Service:** Technicians may occasionally address minor vehicle issues at no charge, recognizing the loyalty and trust you've placed in them. This goodwill can result in free repairs or adjustments that might otherwise have cost you.
- **Expedited Service:** Dispatchers might prioritize your vehicle, ensuring it's in and out of the service department more swiftly. Your trusted status as a customer becomes a catalyst for efficient service delivery.

I have witnessed and have done all 3 myself as a manager, technician, and dispatching.

A Sense of Trust

Trust is the cornerstone of any lasting relationship. When you develop a relationship with your local dealership, you're essentially building a foundation of trust. This trust extends to their advice, recommendations, and the work they perform on your vehicle.

Tailored Service

One of the key advantages of a dealership relationship is the ability to receive service that is tailored to your unique needs and preferences. When your service advisor knows your history and understands your vehicle's quirks, they can recommend services and repairs that genuinely align with your vehicle's requirements.

Loyalty Rewarded

A strong relationship with your dealership can be a two-way street. Just as you remain loyal to them, they often reciprocate by offering loyalty programs, exclusive perks, and priority scheduling for their trusted customers.

Tips for Building a Relationship

Creating a positive relationship with your local dealership doesn't happen overnight. Here are some tips to get you started:

- **Regular Service:** Consistently service your vehicle at the same dealership to establish familiarity.
- **Open Communication:** Maintain open and transparent communication with your service advisor. Share your concerns, ask questions, and express your expectations. Feel free to make small talk as well as we all need that on our day.
- **Respect and Courtesy:** Treat the dealership staff with respect and courtesy. Kindness goes a long way in building lasting relationships.
- **Feedback:** Provide constructive feedback when necessary. This helps the dealership improve its services and shows that you're invested in the relationship. Feedback, bad or good should always be welcomed.

Beyond Cost Savings

While financial benefits are undoubtedly enticing, the true value of a dealership relationship extends far beyond mere cost savings. It encompasses peace of mind, trust, and the knowledge that your vehicle is in capable hands.

A Partnership for the Road Ahead

In conclusion, creating a relationship with the people at your local dealership is akin to forming a partnership for the road ahead.

It's about establishing trust, enjoying personalized service, and reaping financial benefits that can make vehicle ownership a more rewarding experience. So, take the first step, introduce yourself, and nurture a relationship that will serve you well in the world of dealership service. Keep in mind a negative relationship can have the opposite effect.

CHAPTER 9: ASK QUESTIONS AND MAKE THE REPAIR MAKE SENSE: EMPOWER YOURSELF THROUGH KNOWLEDGE

In the realm of vehicle repairs, knowledge is not only empowering but also a key driver of informed decision-making. This chapter explores the art of asking questions when faced with a repair, demystifying the complexities of modern automobiles, and gaining a deeper understanding of the work being performed on your vehicle. By actively participating in the repair process, you become a more informed and empowered vehicle owner.

The Power of Inquiry

When your vehicle requires repairs, it's not just an opportunity to address a mechanical issue; it's also a chance to expand your knowledge about your car. Asking questions is the gateway to understanding the intricacies of your vehicle's systems and the necessity of the repair.

Start with the Basics

Begin your inquiry with the basics. Even if you have limited knowledge about automobiles, you can still ask fundamental questions:

- **What Part Needs Replacement:** Start by asking what specific part requires replacement. Understanding the component involved is the first step in grasping the nature of the repair.
- **How Does It Work:** Delve into the functioning of the part. Ask your service advisor to explain how it contributes to the overall operation of your vehicle.

The Event Leading to the Repair

Dig deeper by inquiring about the events that led to the need for the repair. Understanding the cause is essential:

- **What Happened:** Ask for a detailed account of what occurred to trigger the issue. This insight can help you prevent similar problems in the future.
- **Why Did It Happen:** Seek an explanation of why the issue arose. Was it due to wear and tear, a specific event, or a combination of factors?

The Repair Process

Understanding the repair process itself is crucial. Ask questions related to how the repair will be carried out:

- **How Will It Be Fixed:** Request an explanation of the repair procedure. This can include the steps involved and the tools and techniques used.

- **Duration of the Repair:** Inquire about the estimated duration of the repair. Knowing how long you'll be without your vehicle can help you plan accordingly.
- **Technician Qualifications:** Ask about the technician's qualifications and experience in handling this type of repair.

Alternatives and Necessity

Question the necessity of the repair and explore potential alternatives:

- **Is It Essential:** Ask whether the repair is critical for the safe and efficient operation of your vehicle or if it's more of an optional improvement.
- **Are There Alternatives:** Inquire if there are alternative solutions, such as refurbished parts or aftermarket options, that might be more cost-effective.

Cost Breakdown

Request a detailed cost breakdown of the repair, including:

- **Parts Costs:** Understand the costs associated with the replacement parts.
- **Labor Charges:** Inquire about the labor charges involved in the repair, including the hourly rate and estimated labor hours.
- **Additional Costs:** Ask about any additional fees, such as diagnostic charges or disposal fees.

The Long-Term Impact

Consider the long-term impact of the repair:

- **Future Preventative Measures:** Seek advice on preventative maintenance or measures you can take to reduce the likelihood of a similar issue occurring in the future.
- **Also ask about the warranty on the repair.** Most OEM parts have a warranty along with the installation.

Building Knowledge Over Time

Remember that building knowledge about your vehicle is an ongoing process. Each repair or service visit provides an opportunity to expand your understanding. Document what you learn to build a valuable resource for future reference.

The Benefits of Being Informed

By actively engaging in the repair process through questions, you not only gain knowledge but also ensure that the repair makes sense to you. This knowledge empowers you to make informed decisions about your vehicle's maintenance and repairs, ultimately contributing to a more satisfying and cost-effective ownership experience.

A Journey of Empowerment

In conclusion, asking questions and seeking to make the repair process comprehensible is a journey of empowerment as a vehicle owner. It transforms a seemingly daunting repair into a learning opportunity, allowing you to take charge of your vehicle's well-being and make informed choices that align with your needs and budget. So, never hesitate to ask questions, for knowledge is the key to making the repair process not just manageable but meaningful.

CHAPTER 10: ASK WHAT THEY WOULD DO TO THEIR OWN CAR OR THEIR MOTHER'S

In the intricate realm of vehicle maintenance and repair, trust is an invaluable currency. Among the arsenal of questions, you can wield to assess the credibility of your service advisor, there's one that carries exceptional weight: "What would the technician do if this were your own car or your mother's?"

A Question That Holds the Key

As a vehicle owner, you often encounter a barrage of advice and recommendations when your vehicle requires servicing or repairs. In this sea of information, the ability to distinguish sound counsel from opportunistic suggestions is vital. This question serves as a litmus test, a key to unlocking valuable insights into your service advisor's dedication to your best interests.

An Illustrative Real-Life Example

Imagine finding yourself faced with a challenging situation involving your vehicle. The service advisor presents you with a repair estimate that seems daunting, and you're wrestling with the decision. In this very moment, a service manager or advisor who's genuinely concerned about your well-being would consider various facets before rendering advice. A real-life example elucidates this concept profoundly.

A customer arrives at the dealership with an issue—her vehicle's Engine/Powertrain Control Module sporadically triggers an error code, but only in the morning at first start up. The manufacturer's recommendation prescribes a substantial repair that could potentially cost thousands of dollars. Understandably, the customer is anxious about the financial implications and inquiries about payment plans.

However, as she presents her frustrations and money issues I dove deeper into the situation. After I got all the details and me having a technician background able to get more involved with the diagnostics I asked as always what I would do to my vehicle or my mother's. Could there be other factors at play? Is there a simpler, more cost-effective solution? In this instance, I shared my perspective—before jumping into the expensive repair, I suggested changing the oil using the correct type. As this code was setting for a system that is oil controlled and we have no record of this vehicles history and do not know what oil is in it.

Performing an oil change clearing the code and monitoring the situation might be the wiser course of action. After all, modern vehicles are equipped with ultra-sensitive computer systems that can trigger check engine lights for minor glitches. In essence, this advice mirrors what I would do if it were my own vehicle or my mother's. For this case the code was monitored in milliseconds and when watching data, you could not even see it happen. There was a bulletin to make a 2k dollar repair. After digging into this I recommended what I would do to my vehicle, and she was so relieved. Especially since the vehicle went awhile before she stopped in again to say thanks and tell me the light had not come back on. The 2k dollar repair was justifiable to fix the issue, but it was not 2k I would have spent right away. Just remember the answer to this question should come from the technician as he will know much better.

Trusting the Advisor's Judgment

This approach underscores a service advisor's commitment to your best interests. They treat your vehicle as they would their own or their mother's, factoring in pragmatism, necessity, and cost-effectiveness. It's a demonstration of trustworthiness—a pledge to provide solutions that resonate with your unique needs and circumstances.

The Value of Pragmatism

In today's rapidly evolving automotive landscape, not every illuminated check engine light demands an immediate, costly response. Modern vehicles boast intricate computer systems that can signal minor hiccups or transient issues. When such scenarios arise, a pragmatic perspective can save both time and money. As a Master ASE and 100% GM trained technician I can say my check engine light has been on for a while and because I know what it is I am in no rush to fix it, and it's cheap. That is one thing to keep in mind us technicians may slack in some repairs on their vehicle as they are known for. We always keep up with maintenance but if the repair is not truly needed, we will probably hold off. I know techs driving vehicles with 350k+ miles on them.

Empowering Vehicle Owners

As a vehicle owner, you wield the power to pose this question and gauge the authenticity of the advice you receive. When confronted with a substantial repair estimate or a perplexing issue, do not hesitate to inquire how the service technician would navigate the situation if it were their own vehicle or their mother's.

The Essence of Trust in Vehicle Service

In essence, this question encapsulates the trust that should underpin your relationship with a service advisor. Trust forms the bedrock of a successful and satisfying service experience. By asking what your service technician would do in a similar situation, you gain valuable insights into their commitment to your best interests.

A Service Advisor Worth Sticking With

If you encounter a service advisor who answers this question with integrity and transparency, consider it a partnership worth nurturing. A service advisor who treats your vehicle as they would their own or their mother's is an advisor who genuinely has your best interests at heart.

In summation, the question of what a service technician would do to their own car or their mother's is a powerful tool for vehicle owners. It enables you to make informed decisions and build trust with your service department. Ultimately, it leads to a service experience that is not only reliable but also aligned with your unique needs and circumstances—a true testament to the benefits of fostering a lasting relationship with your service department.

www.ingramcontent.com/pod-product-compliance
Lightning Source LLC
Chambersburg PA
CBHW062305290526
45794CB00006B/2703